HARROW

ELIZABETH ROBINSON

Omnidawn
Richmond, California
2001

Other Books
by Elizabeth Robinson:
In the Sequence of the Falling Things
Bed of Lists
House Made of Silver

ACKNOWLEDGEMENTS
The author would like to express her appreciation to the following magazines
in which some of these poems (or versions thereof) first appeared:
*Abacus, American Letters & Commentary, Angle, Antenym, Apex of the M, Caliban,
First Intensity, New American Writing, Oblek, Outlet,* and *Talisman.*

Thanks are extended to the editors of *Primary Trouble: an anthology of contemporary
american poetry* (Talisman House) and *The Gertrude Stein Awards in Innovative
American Poetry 1993-1994* (Sun & Moon) for including poems in this collection
in their anthologies.

I would like to give particular thanks to Leonard Brink of Instress Press for
publishing several of these poems in a chapbook, *Other Veins, Absent Roots,* and
Andrew Mossin of Quarry Press for publishing *As Betokening.* Their support of
my work has meant a great deal to me.

Rusty Morrison collaborated with me to make this book a coherent whole.
Her attentiveness to these poems and their relationship to each other has made
this a much stronger book than it might otherwise have been. My heartfelt
thanks to her.

Book cover and interior design by Philip Krayna Design, Berkeley, California.

Cover illustration by Marianne Kolb, *Puccini Café Imagination, No.3,* expresso,
sugar, and graphite on Abaca paper.

Published by Omnidawn Publishing, Richmond, California
www.omnidawn.com · (800) 792-4957

ISBN: 1-890650-07-2 (paper)   9 8 7 6 5 4 3 2 1

Printed in the United States on recycled paper.

Table of Contents

PART ONE

Apollo

I know the way the funnel works. The part of the fact seen
between columns. Gibberish unearthed from dirt. Mother
and husband.

I know you were proximate. Assign me the Ion. The flaw
of grace is proof. Stones become restless too, tired of being
encoded, a trinity. But a temple should carry the memory
of narrative.

The mothering hand falls to the shoulder, architecture.
Her act is secured, the garment discarded, the gown obdurate.
Profligate. She has not committed the reading to its proper
time. The rape buried in the hill and its lateness.

We always hear her voice from the other room, overburdening
our married life. I have my hand to your jaw, finger over
tongue. A boy would grow up. So you should succumb, that
I talk jerkily, my foreign way. That he has been reassigned to
me; wreathing.

For this, the lady takes her shovel in hand and buries the
instruments of the cloth. There is irony to legitimacy,
tiredness.

I ask as if I were the one to be recognized. A pressure of
utterance, he then came forward in drapery pieced together
from their unearthings. A god's body formed in the
translation, viscous aftereffect of speaking.

Experience

I try to defend the orthodoxy of the icon, of uranos and gaia:
Any sane person can compare. But, heretic,
you move among the forms of illogic while the form speaks
    to you.
Where vision precedes hearing. Can't the form
of the evangel be reborn alike in eclipse?

Or hypostasis:
What is created, like a word, is circumscribed, a man in the
form of the moon
with all his singular deformities—
simultaneous in time, God and God, the word in its state
    of experience
is never spoken.
But we do act, visually, to remember its timelessness.

Then the question: You find a space,
heretic, whose width conveys meaninglessness.
The prod of that glow in memory.
The womb,
like groping the moon, opens to creatures and the son of man
has no size.
A desire created by seeing and impiety,
in this case, becomes the object of its own lunar orbit, perhaps,
worthy of veneration.

Plaid

i.
To engineer traffic
is to move in one's sleep.

"I cried out":
this is a pattern, too,

& the billboard functions as sudden
and useful mirror.

Intersection, intercourse,
interdict, intermittent,
pause introduction.

ii.
What matters most is to appear tidy.
I see it in the bloodstream,

arteries translucent
with orderly movement.

To be faithful, properly,
is to be transparent via this.

iii.
"A" Street crosses 1st Avenue
and so on.

Gingham or plaid. So
fortunate that the steering
wheel

insists on circularity.   ·

Interference, interlocutor,
intelligence, interruption,
rupture, internal, rapture.

Rapt, raptor.

Twirl the rapacious skirt
on the seat beside you. I take
direction, maplike.

Clad in stripes, by-ways' boulevards.

iv.
Ridden until the route
is glossy.

"I subside": not a weaver
but a designer of 'substance'"

woof

and warp themselves,
this matter

of locomotion.

Haste, intercity,
we wear our transport.

Delightful texture, threads, each, in place.

v.
And reverse to the underside:
"I mumble":

interest, intermix, interfaith,
impertinent, lagging

opaque.   As one goes home
automatically

to draw blankets and shades
neatly up or down

squared frames.
Interceding for bodies.   Them.

Cleared to the point of iridescence.

Uprising

This leaf is impotent
by one whom its gloss receives.

But then, this marker is a picture of myself,
leaded between pieces of glass.

The mute coating of these many cells
hardens in response to its articulation

like paths of frequented truths
or well-circulated air.

A tree, then,
to counter so many other veins of reproduction.

There is a new method of sleep
which softens the bones of the face

like hands brushing hair toward the icon, then back.

Tree

Its reversal,

he could say—

Pallor became

the forbidden image.

An inscription in the pocket

sloping outward.

All gold; digressive splinters.

All the force of the body to the body
some requirements need.

But it was a trunk
that engorged his lungs.

Some codes elongate.

For some, he knew to blaspheme,

the chips clinging to the axe.

A base for prolongation.

Nailed the slushy boards together.

Slats and tines.

Adherences
from which the line slacks.

Built a neck that stuck in grief of the fork.

Hid time.

The peak of the aftereffect
holds his study.

A regular casement for mercy

he runs alongside.

What is the purport of the wood
conjures the prohibited to its eyes.

War
makes a tardy charge into the sap.

If the rim
could come—

the bough, logical,
and sever
curvature, disobedience
made too obvious.

Adversity was his underbelly.

A word
in a man

climbs up
this scrawniness,

emendation.

He could worship the voice through the
    door:

image or the grain

on a table infuriated.

The next day he planted his foot

in the head; its shadow

spat vigorously.

The house, too, upended.   And consoled

him inside it,

that there
a grove rode brass and angry.

How the trees will compete.   The cluster
settled in dust

confirmed
the coating

put on this memory.

If it were all over the trees, the cowlicks,
the sussurations.

Told this lie before.

The perils are put on their marks and run.

This was a canopy, but

the hard column of its gaze . . .

All an arrow
was unmeeting,

precipitate.

He was gathering up

aim and palpitating,

it's said.

A sort of politic,
more and more trees

and all asunder.

A dry laugh, a cough.   Hush
each whorl on the pavement.

This had a spur on it.

Snowed off

faith

reverted on impact.

Air on this target carbonated

fossilized bloom.

This is an artifact of recall.

On its shoulder there's a sack of retrievals

and the twigs nest there.

All to the baked material of suspension
in this pod—

and this worm hung by its ringed mouth.

A base forged circles inside the rim it was
his idea to climb,

shimmy up the opaque material and pluck.

If it were not so lunar a foliage
that hung down acquisitive.

White paste painted around the middle.
Warning.   He was thickening.

Eye upon the transparency that proved the
color of the eye.

A trunk, a hand's span.
This shadow dangled, upside down,
gave respite

from heat.   In that way.   Warding off light.
Daubed his sayings

with leaves.   Plastered over the hive

with skin.
He heard that.   Insupportable, the
          electricity

of the bosk.

He reversed direction from within.

Heels at ears.

The bough in the arm

in dun's molestation.

A shrew's skin.

If the root harrows,

what gratitude

would sharpen the line there was—
There was not a shadow, but

on the morning a response ran from it.

Temple of the Mariposa

We have seen what simplicity can do.
At the very base of the ledge is a set of stairs
which lead us back down again.   The fields
overridden by weeds
choke our abandoned platform.
We know the reclaimers
and their inability to think above noise and mineral.
Up on the lintel, we carve in the shape of ash.
And then invisible snow.
By the edge we thought there was a pool beneath us.
What is horrible in this mechanism
is the sound of its attachment.   When the descent stops,
the absence irritates us.
Steal, then, and return the green of the mediation.
Return to us the pool while it rolls down the stair.
Affection is steep but not complicated.
And the angles.   And reverence of highways.
We have adoration
of struggle—And the bridge
scratched off underground paintings.

Slope

These few queries
at last

beneath a shower of unknown
substance

ask how one fares
or is formed,

lingering.

You were gone
in resemblance

to night
and all contradiction

aside diction.

Before I attach
to any object

or regain sight,

what charge?
No one

is here to give instruction.

Something is read

and then,
there,

a pause for response.

A single mourner gives it.

Lost arrangement

will perdure elsewhere.

All progress is untimely,

the antiphon taught to

be its shadow. How you fare, or will,

what your regular substance is

at its leaving off point.

Saying

He carried the chair out
to the attestation of daylight.
That which is given, like a girl's name,
Clara. He travels toward this.
Not knowing the scales
or the lathered senses hewing.

Morning glories are stitched into
the warning, slowly, a distress
that choreographs. A chair, elevated,

recombinant, is due the respect of age. The chain links, the
shushing of dogs—solidly affirm
an exterior current. To move

but not to look, borealis, at the
city, just off— This, from now on,
will be a glassine frame. As he gets up
and walks to work in effort.

He does carry the chair onto the stage
as though its soul would have such sheen
manipulating light.

The eclipse's propulsion to labor.
His daughter, Grace, partially named,
uses filters to look at the shadow.

Mortar

Beholden or enlarged,
this mosaic,
its plaiting mid-entry
makes me follow.

My uneven center, its mortar
comprehends the way, its pleasure
in the single tile.

Enlarged and, now, unlettered,
the pattern cannot redeem its
visceral spelling.

Light enters the stomach,
reverting to the eyes whose
ceramic patterns

won't be burned.
They can turn and expose.

To prefer the inadvertent, to recognize
nausea as more than illness, its new circuitry.

What passes for guidance, chip by chip,

can illumine the fatigue
strewn in this path
of nourishment and flint.

Happenstance: Landscape

i.
Perfect arch
that tugs air and
ground into each the other's mouth.
No need to breathe now.   A memory
of that great river trained through the awning.

No permission for memory
but doubt and confidence
loiter.   Two winged creatures
make a spiral over the dead lawn.

Years later
grief can be molded
into a waxy figure, not enormous,
but able to bear weight.

A green hill, huge, I imagined
never existed.   Its arts overtook me
then I overturned it.   Exotic boat.
I could.   Who could hold something in
hand, torturing space.

ii.
You see the sails.   I want you
to see the masonry.   Removed
geography makes these hived
arches watertight.   You see
how precisely you will become
my equivalent.

Nothing decorative can remain,
but still the pleasure, the singing, even
flawed sounds.   Boom and clatter.

Something warm surges
around my shins.   Then, the ground rubbed
hard would yield.   Brazen.
I would not yield.
Debt's tide
a seeming finality—the crown.

PART TWO

As Betokening

A Note

i.

To profess faith, to shrug off its obligations, to enter or
abjure community, to nurture doubt, to force the twain
to come together—two miscreant children tugged by their
ears until face to face. Twins, simultaneously they close their
eyes. Refuse to see the reflection. A world pools around
them. Sunlight comes down hard on them. And girls, no
less, they shouldn't be fighting, little hooligans.

To put on tradition like a daily uniform, unattractive
but reasonably comfortable. To don tradition like a
cast-off costume, newly exoticized. To loosen the collar
and find oneself walking in the world unclad. Naked and
uncomfortably doubled.

These poems are a story. I began them on the figurative
eve of my entry into what became a protracted theological
education. From that site, I began to read scriptural texts,
apocrypha, pseudopigrapha. The beautiful awkwardness
of the language often entranced me. The figures and their
miracles, the attestations against all reason, the unreadable
clichés, the transgressions, so many, branching out: sinners
willing transcendence, radiant, then fallen into a paltry
grasping for order and control.

This poem struggles with that transgressive will, that
bullheaded will tethered as it is, on the one hand to a
faith and faith's attendant tenderness for the open door
of language and, on the other, with the real but unstable
value, the unbearable constraint of tradition's grammar.

Faith and skepticism chain me to my will, foster a generative ambivalence. This is what poetry says: faith is uneasy, an erotic uncertainty. Poetry makes faith out of willed attention. The word is its own commitment, willful for its own sake, a poltergeist who hunts out its double in order that their gaze may be shared. That reciprocity is a kind of cancellation. Their met line of sight is a line of melody made static and dissonant, only just suggesting a small trueness between the converging, diverging vibrations. That is to say: here is a polemic, but not one imposed from an outside.

ii.

In the Cluny Museum in Paris, there is a small statue of the
Virgin. In one arm, she carries the Christ child, in the other
what I presume to be Eve's apple. That opposition would
seem to say enough.

But there's more! Hinges permit her outer self to part and
open. Inside, one finds God himself, his head implanted in
her abdomen; he is seated in her hips. With his hands he
holds up the crucified Christ. God looks worn and worried.
Mary's face, above this, conveys a wise pleasure, almost a
smugness. And to either side, under the protective umbrella
of her downturned palms, congregants look on. Reverent,
grieving, curious, bland, doubtful. Perhaps what they are
really viewing is each other.

The body. The desire for freedom and for order's abolition
of chaos. An interminable search all within the accepted-
for-the-sake-of-argument body. No tradition abides forever.
No exile lasts forever. Some unexpected hinges swing the
doors open and the parties gape at the discrepancy, mostly
in relief.

As Betokening
Prelude

That the cornerstone,
this air, she found, caused

that the granite appeared to be
dawning.
The impact of the neck as it arched forward.

She found that the letters grew larger
was it

a warm push, a warm push.
Overhead, apparently, dawn she found

whose footsteps creaking midboard.

i.
The system of apostrophe
inside a dry portrait.

A halo stood in coarse hair,
its word longing for use.

This:

she-queen wry and gold in
the pattern, floral,
its system of duos, pairs

and the claws broken off all her royal
fingertips.

Systemic
as illness once was in symmetry.

ii.
After ascension, this Item strode down the steps
and leavened the bread that propelled her.   Faith.   We
had known her as the mercury fish that darted
on the wood's floor,
                    but did we know she could fly.

The dough would not rise, so she called out a younger
(some ascribe this to her youngest) daughter. Would
the paste cover her hands. She completed the task.

All the time we were contributors, aghast in the cold,
at the blankets we held around ourselves she understood
as betokening her radiance.

iii.

She then said, "I will tell you what the [word indecipherable] will not tie," but her method of divination was, visibly, not proper. It was, again, a daughter who stood behind her face.

She says, "I'm waiting."

We began to need to know how many progeny there had been. Wisdom. But, except airborne, their titlings came too large for us.

She wanted to know herself how to build a fire and we could not find it in our hearts but to refuse the request.

Appendages the animal doesn't have.

Pseudopodium.

iv.
Saw her who had affronted
the Mystery.

It
by a certain welling of the eyes.

They by now
have tumbled
downward this slope.

The scope of the look askance.

Switch the track
to accommodate the compass.

Lay of diversions.

v.
But there was beauty in this excuse,
a band brought

around the forehead,
the lips,

had sewn out any tension.

Unsought fecundity,
pendant from around the neck
of the bridal garment.

Not lawful for this presence to mourn.

vi.
Rolling over, tannic and tea-colored,
the waist glassy.   If it had been
denoted by gender, it would have
been a 'female'.   Not that she
was in any way essential.   *This is a piece*

It might snap threads of document
between its teeth at the errant
tenancy.   It does have this might.

Suddenly ready after protracted withdrawal.
A brew, it does have this.

Said: even if all, not I.

Said: that shall twice bay and thou
Said: Before it bay twice today

first shalt thrice
thou shalt thrice

vii.
The primary several dimensions of shapes in a bright occult.
When she was born, no one observed her birth.   But later,
afterward, they recalled having celebrated

involuntarily.   The other, a boy, born in honey,
moth-consumer of the woven, a stainer of waters.

She lives through peculiar dishonor, a worshiper of
parted water, and in that series of days when ink
was not amenable to fluid composition.   And the 'he'
of reference dabbles his toes in it, throwing them up.
Wetting her from the shore.   Earlier, Miriam.

Now the skirt of the whole 'island' was already covered,
who widowed, legitimately divorced, was allowed to return
to paternal feast.   The light eats regardless of the law.

Still.

The memory is warted. Of childhood contentment, the images
that appear just before sleep.   Chasteness
did not necessitate arrows.
They could see each other from across the field and she
was astride the gap.

As to say her offering was a complete unwillingness.

Her 'names of the patriarchs' are not the members of the soul.
Even the omission counters what underlies this suggestion:

all ye in this
night shall be offended according to
the scripture

and it wants sparseness, the herb in saltwater, compelling her
to sit on the third step.

What makes order within itself, more profoundly than
irrelevance.
To throw light upon.
An act whose name was 'forgetfulness.'
—by this one list we undo death.

Each enumerated item, let it take, every one, a lamp,
and let it be burning, that the child not turn backward
and her heart be templed away from captivity.

viii.
Mother of a stoning,
where gold might substitute for this grave misunderstanding
(within appointed time).

Conjure
sibilants: snake, Sabbath, resting in sadness.

And cream poured from overhead, exacerbating
the praise.

Unarrowed base
and the shaft of the bird imitating manna, the blasphemer

teeth like a flock just

shorn

coming up

from washing,

head drenched from each direction. It was hers.

ix.
Covered cold with tongue

    and the trunks creak.

On a hill, a mound—

    nerve in pulpit;
    white birch distresses its skin.

                     She tied

the stranger.
Later saw him and merged

as her twin, her brother and her self.

x.

*Five of you will chase a hundred and a hundred of you will
chase ten thousand.*
                    —*Leviticus 26:8*

What will bring you sudden terror in a shrinking script.
There's a device which commits murder.   Resides on a hill
with a house.   Place a jar of sugar on the doorstep and
the house collapses.

Take away the jar and bring soup.   Sweep off the step.
Your enemies will eat it.   Your roads will be deserted.

Flies over. It sees the skeleton carved in the chalk.
She sees the ten women who bake bread in one oven.

Devoted:
the irrevocable giving over of things, often by means
of total destruction.

xi.
She crawled into the tumor of the tree, safe there.

The baby walked out from inside her, her xiphoid blossoming.

Coughed up.

The nesting bird says: I have talked to you before; now
    I am abrupt.
She says: I am impatient too.

From a distance it looked deceptively as though a man
    stood behind.
That his branches wrapped her snugly, from behind.   But
then it could be seen that it was a dress, blue rubbed into the
horizon.

xii.
Prepared

a bottle of warping formula.

This she overcame,

that the word was so strong

—a squiggle.   She read

into the same fugue: Clank

Thud   Rain

So many slappings of the wet boughs,

if it were possible that the single is woman,
should never die.

xiii.
She lay eastward

       and got up and was arrayed
       in the stutter: Sup   Supply

And she turned:

       was it supple uttered

       A corporeal leap

of variable lengths, her soul

       into the bosom of her sun.

White as snow.
And the mistaken word was snow.

xiv.
Do not remove the airborne.   Do not remove the poles.
It is wrong to hurry.   She would sleep here on the porch,
all summer, straining the muscles of her belly.
Do not apply this face to yourself.   That snail
leaves her trail.   Forbear to look at the porch again.

She is hungry now, the moment excessive by
refraction.   Sometimes, in the summer, she sleeps
in the coliseum.   The steps of her stage cover
this moss.   Don't erase the record of this, please.
There was a clash, of course, a white object and
blank one.

xv.
Now to commit silence.   A drink of anything
for the thirsty.   Nought.   Nought to be distributed

anywhere.   Now to impute the feminine onto this
     four letters. Onto.
Cones and rods, these are soots caught in the eye.
Unblinded, and here a drink of water would desecrate
     the dead body with love.

That earliest infancy I ingest moves in unison with each
sound. The opposites of the war that can only imply a drink
of mourning water.

xvi.
That has pryingness
cracking shells.

A beak, nipping.　　Remember

a different equanimity—
a spiral bridge,
skipping the guidance line

and wrinkling the shell.
　　　　　　　　.

　　But this biting of pests
in embryonic pulses.

　　She does this still—
to the work, the net
work.

　　But this husk cutting back
inattentive with coercion.

xvii.
A portion carved out of atmosphere
by glare.

It had a cap
that sifted one into another,
wet and dry,

until temperature does not pertain.

A cap, a robe.
A finer patience

who was sturdy and leaf-bitten,
vibrating away from its gravity.

xviii.
Set in the dark, gradually, not in fear
but because the process of the night
is so fragile.   The padding of many
sheets pressed down by what we'd
want to be a stylus.

Dimly incurring a debt.

Always a tea to be steeping, that
powerful legs could wade through.

It was a rock thrower, a giantess,
whose recipient caught the rock
and then entered it.

An overlapping bludgeon which
held her garments in piece,
gave the jailer a silver mirror.

xix.
Inside the burl and humming, faintly, a tune.
There was an image in that sphere who
made the wasp buzz around.

Next a glass casement held the figure
and that figure was then made to remove
its drapery.   Not to madden the insects
and be stung by the form's spice.

Made to avoid sleep in captivity, so
exhaustion suffused its skin and dyed its flesh.
In the way of the radish, white inside.

An image that rolled across the supernal floor
while other legs of the *image* motivated the globe.

xx.
Lift the hazard
and lift the

curtain.   The possible hasp.

Hazard this lisping
unshod.

Sleep, fidget the lock
who'll have gotten away.

Hands for sleep,
honey, ulna—

Finger dipped in
carpal, metacarpal.

And possible:
do not overcome.

xxi.
As if I were not able to endure

this marbling tears swatches of itself and

deformation of paper makes bone.

The mural of truth mimics the horizon, burning in a hedge.

xxii.
Kindly, to bury the body who attends it.
A model of her house frosted over the cake.

And eaten, rough over mild.

On suspicion.   On epiphany.
It multiplies in the gullet,
shuffling all the loose dirt back and forth
across the pathway.

xxiii.
Her movement's abreaction
took census.

Her toes met, her heels parted—
kuh-nock kuh-need—
were required to warn

throughout encampments.

Any bed her pelvis touched,
each bisection her shins met
            unclean until evening.

The clay shattered, but
            the wood, the leprous pallor, the brass
held under, washed, water, the herald questioning.

That fouled emission of
infinite points' series.

xxiv.
No reference today—

but the funnel
a lake presses about the neck.

A release of livid color
shearing the hair, a stolen lie.

Then selling it to the priest's fire
as nearby a crowd with staves
all drowning the razor.

xxv.
A machinery insists on such garb
                    disburdening
                    the pollen of devils.

Stretching laundry over the drumhead,
                    basin of congestion.
                    It was a filter

of outlandish fumes, funnels, dust, batons, comedy, paces,
patterns immemorial.

xxvi.
Two circles overlapping make the slot
through which this coin drops.   Then through

the cerise, the maroon, a finger held to the inner corner
of the eye took pulse.

This pleasing loop clattered from the lips
a salute, a pocket of vision, here I am,

on the fringe of which adoration is unmarried.

xxvii.
Noodles, a hairlike formation
—hesitant to permit an adjective: 'lacy'.

Tune going down by fifths; must trill or carol.

Annotated din, or augmented.

Its immolation invoked from the rutilant socket.

xxviii.
The custom of the [synonym] in its whistling.

An arbor: a medieval story
of severance.

Service to the internal organ, a sweet
planted in a sponge

or was it fire announced from the shofar.

Chalcedony and adamant smile, all irregular, baroque,

arraign her.

xxiv.
A desert that replaces the book

in astonished hydration of heaven.

Black mites on the tip of her tongue

who were her preliminary notes

publish the urge bringing sorrow out of this gloss.

PART THREE

Retablo

The rafters themselves smell sweet, pulled

to what they are not,
yet   near.

Imagine a form, living
within that   wooden

      —say it were a self like myself, and I were a humble
      person, often mistaken

for another.

An entity might paint over its being,
natural

dye, tincture, hue

of the roof beam whose cache

(the vertical in favor of the recumbent)—

Holy to lie there, in hiding, and holier
still, to be stolen away

by misuse of purpose.

A wash of cylindrical light
stumbling down

varnished hovel by mistaken

glory.   And they tilted,

clandestinely, and moved in several
directions

as to why the humble choose
to make home in the house with the roof

as was sometimes banished.

Salpiglosis

Yellow veined trumpet
of the core

swarms the heart
that finally represents

a skin peeled effortlessly
off the fingertip

in the day of the gathering.

Enflames

so that chart
of the horn

could still earlier
have stalks.

Have arms around, like the many-jarred
heart of the bee in its

home.
Another reference means

Strayed.   To its veins
an inadvertent layer meandering

to a place once known
as   Voluntary

and prolonged
history.   Who

can have recognized
this knowledge.   These versions

which cling in the print
of the finger.   This scrollwork

put in the hive.   Fine

horn

ingathered.

Appointment

The scent of fading light,
voluminous.
I,
hypothetical
cathedral,
find whitewash
facing me.
We remain who we are,
but slowly,
by insertion.
This plant
gives up its furred leaves,
or the feet
form words unsteadily.
There is no image here
of inevitability,
this woman's hair drifting
in the labyrinth.
This single hair
where the ceiling is so distant.
An improper good-bye
rises out from me
recycled and un-mazed.

Entry for Song

Warning

This is the contour
that I'd deliquesce.
That I'd choose abbreviation.

The tongue is a fire,
a sign painter, incendiary paint.
A vocation.
In I go

where else I'd advertise my trade,
trite and inebriate and bereft
penned aside of this
seeming domicile.

i.
Have I invited you
to mine?

Raise

the chair.
You may reach

with temerity and so

stray.

A posture,
for I shall dwell.

I shall assemble
my cold fingers

for wear
in the house
of my own lagging.

Forever reciting.

I will, mid-point, eat
at a table
set for me.

ii.
Oh what a foretaste.

Cursing beneath the buoyant fruit

for or at

God who would repent

for
or beside

vessel or indigence.

I live in a boat

of glory.

I could pain the water beneath me.

Blessed assurance I'd depict,

crew who will throw

me to see,

scaled belly of these suspect sailors.

iii.
Whatever you ask

will be

where foxes have holes.

And birds,

in this name for air,

will be given to you.

For you are benumbed by this ether

and your soul now resides

in season

at the right hand

of God, camouflaged

scrap on which to lay your head.

iv.
Here on

the ladder

cleft for me:

be of fog

the double cure.

For wrestling with

the nation

on the rung,

it makes my least version

rock

from thy

clouded side.

v.
My darlings

toss me in

whose weak sire

knows me
as far in distance,
his.

Alright,
many stripes drawn from veins

of color—

Aiding hand plunged beneath that flood,

vowed under thigh,

swears all their guilty stains.

vi.
Let me secret

myself

in thee.

In your

tongue

circumcised at

its margin.

Marked with freight

this word

is guarantee

for weeds

washing up

in its true course.

vii.
When I fall

Deborah

on my knees

Jael brings

with my face

milk to the tent.

What was a sanctuary

is a stake.

Have mercy

on that temple, that is

my forehead

breaking together

with bread.

viii.

I come to the garden alone

and pour

on his feet

a misstep of

my own choosing.

Falling to my ear

on the insuring floor:

blanket

the forecast discloses.

Mopping with my hair

mistaken oil,

for his own

are all relative

where we tarry, little known.

ix.
We know this to be a correction

on which all

keep silence.

Falsely ruddy,

bifurcate

passengers misapprehend

themselves for passage

in human vesture.

Streaks,

covenanted
sleepless eye

on this.

Mendicant

When there is a name for a thing and it is injured
by gravity.

This, the surface of the world snags its own script/
ed flesh.

Barely noticeable abrasions, age marks,
calm soil inundated with dew.

And nocturnal rain, dull as

a messianic call

to reach out:

end the arm's itching.

The name is water soluble
and the arm
is too

so that the sound of it, pattering
or scratched—

resumes graceless

and less abrupt.   The languorous body

is merely tired.   The

station at which gestures meet
stumbling   or stealthy.   That continuous

weather, termed for convenience

as ache;   terminus.

Something falls down quite simply
and alights on another thing will

to bear the weight.   This extends

always

to the dullness sought, leaned towards
that saves
up.   Like the name drawn.   The

forearm,   rash
and aimless.   Meant wandering

for spots

in rain's blemish.

Little Book

This periphery tells:

do not be facile.

Self
by clear borders.

Dove in vehement fog.

From the corner of an eye

welling up from this realm of springs.

The reply:

find use.

A gesture over rock in catechesis.
Gesture not to be so simple.

This margin lays itself there
and then returns

to renumber the page.

Wing, to alter the shape of the outermost.

The Circulation

Maybe two birds

are eaten by birdlike waves.

Gold waves on

air,

conditioned and

discarded.

This road itself

breaks in two

at blue and green

which we do not

recognize as machinery

of water and leaf.

Maybe the frame

of the picture

is in a gully

where there are red

veins underneath air,

bird, and machine.